CONCEPTS OF LIBERTY: The Declaration of Independence

U.S. Revolutionary Period | Fourth Grade History
Children's American Revolution History

UNIVERSAL POLITICS
POLITICS & SOCIAL SCIENCES

First Edition, 2020

Published in the United States by Speedy Publishing LLC, 40 E Main Street, Newark, Delaware 19711 USA.

© 2020 Universal Politics Books, an imprint of Speedy Publishing LLC

Universal Politics Books are available at special discounts when purchased in bulk for industrial and sales-promotional use. For details contact our Special Sales Team at Speedy Publishing LLC, 40 E Main Street, Newark, Delaware 19711 USA. Telephone (888) 248-4521 Fax: (210) 519-4043. www.speedybookstore.com

10 9 8 7 6 * 5 4 3 2 1

Print Edition: 9781541950320
Digital Edition: 9781541952126

See the world in pictures. Build your knowledge in style.
www.speedypublishing.com

TABLE OF CONTENTS

What would you do if the law suddenly said everyone who wore a T-Shirt on Thursday must go to prison? You would probably think it was a very unfair and ridiculous law and would hope that no police officer would agree to arrest anyone for something like that. If the police did though, and the government kept mistreating people, you would have a right, even an expectation to overturn such a government. Americans can disagree on many things, but there are several documents that explain what all Americans should unite on and strive towards. One of the founding principles of the United States of America is the right to revolution. This book will discuss the Declaration of Independence, the four self-evident truths it established, and the responsibilities it placed on the government and on its citizens.

American flag during Independence Day on the Hudson River

COMMON SENSE

Even after the American Revolution began, in April of 1775, many people still hoped that the British would recognize the rights of the colonists and they could remain British subjects.

Battle of Bunker Hill, Charlestown Massachusetts, 1775

The colonists wanted a peaceful resolution if possible. As the war lasted longer though, independence became a more and more popular idea.

American Independence Day parade

After all, the king was waging war on them, a war
that seemed to be lasting longer and longer.

*Colonists pulling
down the statue of
King George III*

CARLTON T CHAPMAN

The British were causing significant damage, notably in Virginia and in the naval battle at Maine. It did not seem very likely that such a king, who had even hired foreign soldiers to fight them, would listen to his subjects in the colonies and treat them fairly.

Destruction of Portland Maine by artillery fire from British ships

In January of 1776, a pamphlet titled *Common Sense* was published by a journalist named Thomas Paine.

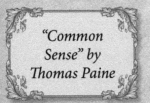

"Common Sense" by Thomas Paine

COMMON SENSE;

ADDRESSED TO THE

INHABITANTS

OF

AMERICA,

On the following interesting

SUBJECTS.

I. Of the Origin and Design of Government in general, with concise Remarks on the English Constitution.

II. Of Monarchy and Hereditary Succession.

III. Thoughts on the present State of American Affairs.

IV. Of the present Ability of America, with some miscellaneous Reflections.

Man knows no Master save creating HEAVEN,
Or those whom choice and common good ordain.

THOMSON.

PHILADELPHIA;

Printed, and Sold, by R. BELL, in Third-Street.

MDCCLXXVI.

Paine wrote the pamphlet to point out all the different ways the king had abused the colonists.

Thomas Paine

The king levied many unfair taxes on the colonies, and hc was too far away to rule them effectively. There was no reason that the colonies should be subject to a king who cared nothing for them and was so far away as to be ineffective.

A cartoon illustration of King George III and Queen Charlotte standing before the Treasury with moneybags under their arms

A meeting of colonists protesting British treatment before the American Revolution.

It would be better if the thirteen colonies formed their own government. Paine thought that creating independent states only made sense.

His fifty pages of writing sold over half a million copies. It went a long way to convincing the colonists that it was time to declare their independence from Britain.

Thomas Paine sold over a million copies of the pamphlet "Common Sense"

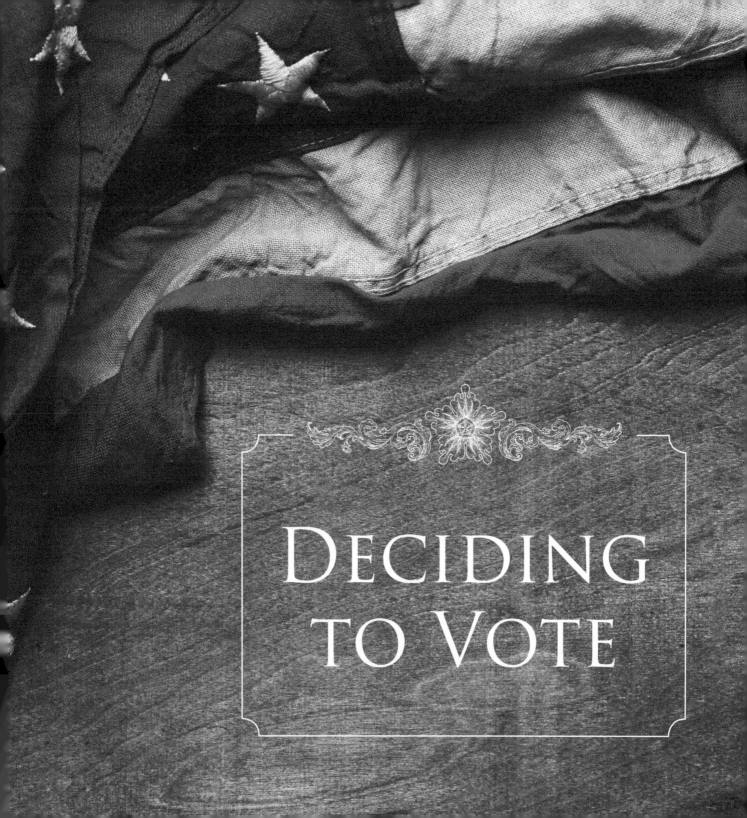

DECIDING TO VOTE

In 1776, by the middle of May, eight of the thirteen colonies had already decided that they would support declaring independence from Britain. When the Continental Congress met for the second time, on June 7, 1776, Richard Lee from Virginia had already been chosen to ask that a formal declaration of independence be considered.

Thirteen colonies decided that they would support declaring independance from Britain

It was agreed that a committee of five people would write a draft. In the end, Thomas Jefferson wrote the first draft with some changes recommended by the other committee members who were Benjamin Franklin, John Adams, Roger Sherman, and Robert R. Livingston.

Thomas Jefferson

Benjamin Franklin

John Adams

Roger Sherman

Robert R. Livingston

Thomas Jefferson burning drafts in the process of perfecting the Declaration of Independence

Jefferson was surprised that he had been asked to write it, as he was one of the youngest members on the committee. He felt John Adams should do it as he had more experience.

However, the other members insisted that Jefferson was the best writer and the best choice. He spent over two weeks working on what would eventually become the Declaration of Independence as we know it.

Benjamin Franklin, John Adams and Thomas Jefferson Drafting the Declaration of American Independence

"The Drafting of the Declaration of Independence"

Since not all of the delegates at the Continental Congress were convinced that reconciliation with Britain was impossible, and other members were not certain if they had permission from their governments to vote on such a significant issue, the Congress took a three-week recess.

This would allow delegates to talk to the people they represented and decide how they should best vote on the idea to declare independence.

Not all of the delegates at the Continental Congress were convinced that reconciliation with Britain was impossible

Thomas Jefferson reading his rough draft of the Declaration of Independence to Benjamin Franklin

It was during this recess that Thomas Jefferson was writing what would become the Declaration of Independence.

The Second Continental Congress would accept the notion of independence on July 2, 1776 and for the next couple of days there were debates about what the declaration should or should not say.

The Second Continental Congress

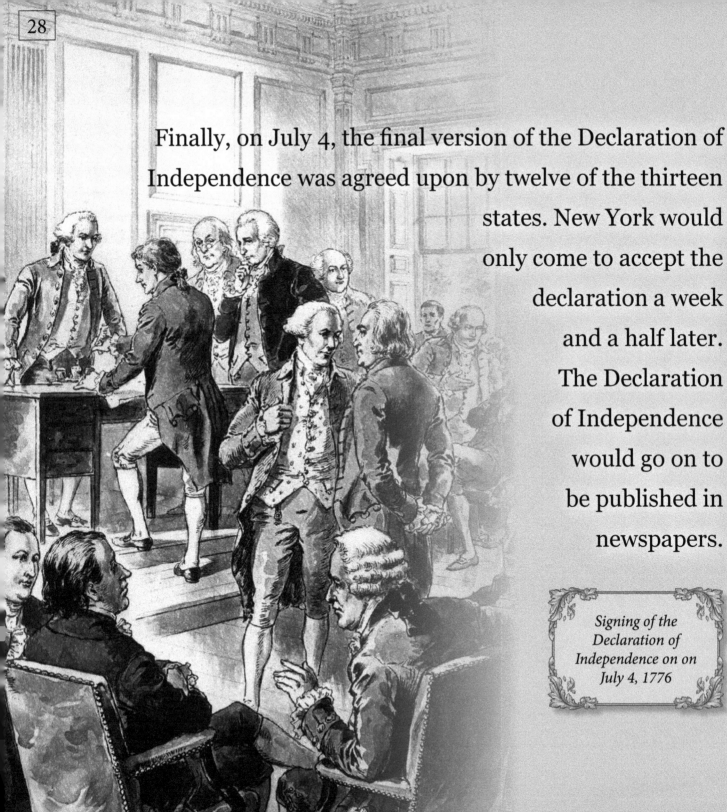

Finally, on July 4, the final version of the Declaration of Independence was agreed upon by twelve of the thirteen states. New York would only come to accept the declaration a week and a half later. The Declaration of Independence would go on to be published in newspapers.

Signing of the Declaration of Independence on on July 4, 1776

It was also read out loud in public all throughout the colonies which had now declared themselves to be independent states. The declaration famously listed twenty-seven issues the former colonists had with King George III.

Reading of the Declaration of Independence in Philadelphia, July 4, 1776

The document then explained that it was precisely this unjust treatment by the British government that would give colonists just cause to declare themselves independent states. Had the American Revolution not succeeded, everyone who had signed the declaration would have been killed for treason against the crown.

United States Declaration of Independence

In CONGRESS, July 4, 1776.

The unanimous Declaration of the thirteen united States of America.

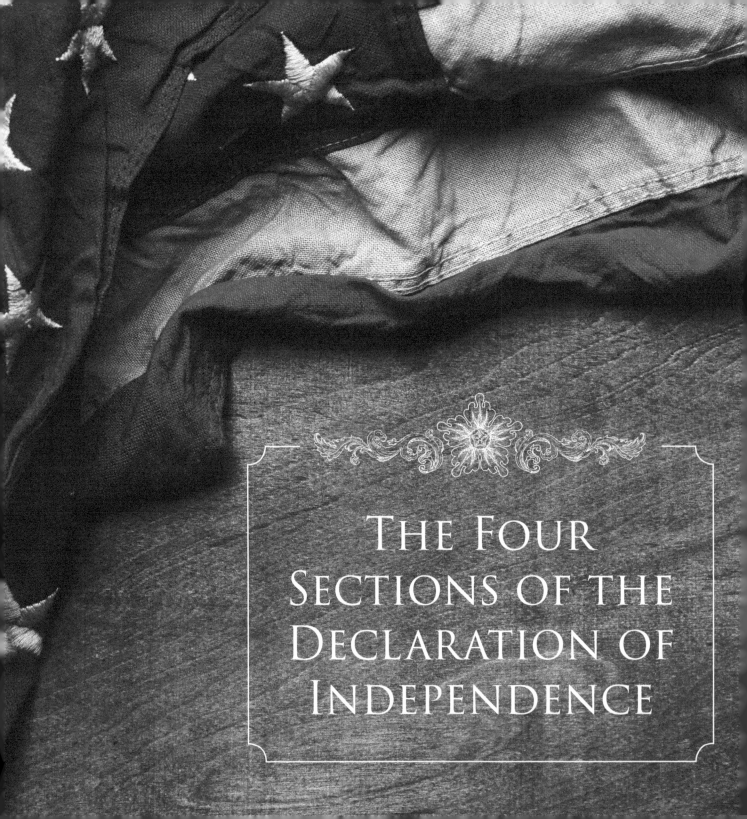

The Four Sections of the Declaration of Independence

The first section is called the preamble. It explains all the reasons why the Americans thought they had to separate from Britain. A preamble is common in legal documents to explain the reason the document was written.

The Preamble

The next is the declaration of rights. This part of the document explains what all people should be allowed to have simply because they are humans. The most well-known are summarized in the right to "life, liberty, and the pursuit of happiness." The Declaration of Independence explained that if any government tried to take these rights away from people, then that government would be at risk of being replaced for failing to protect the rights of the citizens.

IN
CONGRESS,
JULY 4, 1776.

A DECLARATION
BY THE
REPRESENTATIVES
OF THE
UNITED STATES OF AMERICA,
IN GENERAL CONGRESS ASSEMBLED.

WHEN in the Course of human Events, it becomes necessary for one People to dissolve the political Bands which have connected them with another, and to assume among the Powers of the Earth, the separate and equal Station to which the Laws of Nature and of Nature's God entitle them, a decent Respect to the Opinions of Mankind requires that they should declare the Causes which impel them to the Separation.

We hold these Truths to be self-evident, that all Men are created equal, that they are endowed by their Creator with certain unalienable Rights, that among these are Life, Liberty, and the Pursuit of Happiness:—That to secure these Rights, Governments are instituted among Men, deriving their just Powers from the Consent of the Governed, that whenever any Form of Government becomes destructive of these Ends, it is the Right of the People to alter or to abolish it, and to institute new Government, laying its Foundation on such Principles, and organizing its Powers in such Form, as to them shall seem most likely to effect their Safety and Happiness. Prudence, indeed, will dictate that Governments long established should not be changed for light and transient Causes; and accordingly all Experience hath shewn, that Mankind are more disposed to suffer, while Evils are sufferable, than to right themselves by abolishing the Forms to which they are accustomed. But when a long Train of Abuses and Usurpations, pursuing invariably the same Object, evinces a Design to reduce them under absolute Despotism, it is their Right, it is their Duty, to throw off such Government, and to provide new Guards for their future Security. Such has been the patient Sufferance of these Colonies; and such is now the Necessity which constrains them to alter their former Systems of Government. The History of the present King of Great-Britain is a History of repeated Injuries and Usurpations, all having in direct Object the Establishment of an absolute Tyranny over these States. To prove this, let Facts be submitted to a candid World.

He has refused his Assent to Laws, the most wholesome and necessary for the public Good.

He has forbidden his Governors to pass Laws of immediate and pressing Importance, unless suspended in their Operation until his Assent should be obtained; and when so suspended, he has utterly neglected to attend to them.

He has refused to pass other Laws for the Accommodation of large Districts of People, unless those People would relinquish the Right of Representation in the Legislature, a Right inestimable to them, and formidable to TYRANTS only.

He has called together Legislative Bodies at Places unusual, uncomfortable, and distant from the Depository of their public Records, for the sole Purpose of fatiguing them into Compliance with his Measures.

He has dissolved Representative Houses repeatedly, for opposing with manly FIRMNESS his Invasions on the Rights of the People.

He has refused for a long Time, after such Dissolutions, to cause others to be elected; whereby the Legislative Powers, incapable of Annihilation, have returned to the People at large for their Exercise; the State remaining in the mean Time exposed to all the Dangers of Invasion from without, and Convulsions within.

He has endeavoured to prevent the Population of these States; for that Purpose obstructing the Laws for Naturalization of Foreigners; refusing to pass others to encourage their Migrations hither, and raising the Conditions of new Appropriations of Lands.

He has obstructed the Administration of Justice, by refusing his Assent to Laws for establishing Judiciary Powers.

He has made Judges dependent on his Will alone, for the Tenure of their Offices, and the Amount and Payment of their Salaries.

He has erected a multitude of new Offices, and sent hither Swarms of Officers

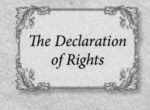

The Declaration of Rights

Another section in the declaration is the list of wrongs. This list spelled out all the harm that was done to the colonists because of the poor actions that were taken by the king. There were twenty-seven items recorded, all of which had occurred between the years of 1763 and 1776. That averages two major wrongs a year.

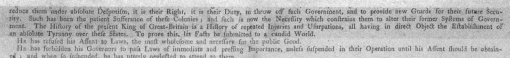

reduce them under absolute Despotism, it is their Right, it is their Duty, to throw off such Government, and to provide new Guards for their future Security. Such has been the patient Sufferance of these Colonies; and such is now the Necessity which constrains them to alter their former Systems of Government. The History of the present King of Great-Britain is a History of repeated Injuries and Usurpations, all having in direct Object the Establishment of an absolute Tyranny over these States. To prove this, let Facts be submitted to a candid World.

He has refused his Assent to Laws, the most wholesome and necessary for the public Good.

He has forbidden his Governors to pass Laws of immediate and pressing Importance, unless suspended in their Operation until his Assent should be obtained; and when so suspended, he has utterly neglected to attend to them.

He has refused to pass other Laws for the Accommodation of large Districts of People, unless those People would relinquish the Right of Representation in the Legislature, a Right inestimable to them, and formidable to TYRANTS only.

He has called together Legislative Bodies at Places unusual, uncomfortable, and distant from the Depository of their public Records, for the sole Purpose of fatiguing them into Compliance with his Measures.

He has dissolved Representative Houses repeatedly, for opposing with manly Firmness his Invasions on the Rights of the People.

He has refused for a long Time, after such Dissolutions, to cause others to be elected; whereby the Legislative Powers, incapable of Annihilation, have returned to the People at large for their Exercise; the State remaining in the mean Time exposed to all the Dangers of Invasion from without, and Convulsions within.

He has endeavoured to prevent the Population of these States; for that Purpose obstructing the Laws for Naturalization of Foreigners; refusing to pass others to encourage their Migrations hither, and raising the Conditions of new Appropriations of Lands.

He has obstructed the Administration of Justice, by refusing his Assent to Laws for establishing Judiciary Powers.

He has made Judges dependent on his Will alone, for the Tenure of their Offices, and the Amount and Payment of their Salaries.

He has erected a multitude of new Offices, and sent hither Swarms of Officers to harrass our People, and eat out their Substance.

He has kept among us, in Times of Peace, Standing Armies, without the Consent of our Legislatures.

He has affected to render the Military independent of, and superior to the Civil Power.

He has combined with others to subject us to a Jurisdiction foreign to our Constitution, and unacknowledged by our Laws; giving his Assent to their Acts of pretended Legislation:

For quartering large Bodies of armed Troops among us:

For protecting them, by a mock Trial, from Punishment for any Murder which they should commit on the Inhabitants of these States:

For cutting off our Trade with all Parts of the World:

For imposing Taxes on us without our Consent:

For depriving us, in many Cases, of the Benefits of Trial by Jury:

For transporting us beyond Seas to be tried for pretended Offences:

For abolishing the free System of English Laws in a neighbouring Province, establishing therein an arbitrary Government, and enlarging its Boundaries, so as to render it at once an Example and fit Instrument for introducing the same absolute Rule into these Colonies.

For taking away our Charters, abolishing our most valuable Laws, and altering fundamentally the Forms of our Governments:

For suspending our own Legislatures, and declaring themselves invested with Power to legislate for us in all Cases whatsoever.

He has abdicated Government here, by declaring us out of his Protection and waging War against us.

He has plundered our Seas, ravaged our Coasts, burnt our Towns, and destroyed the Lives of our People.

He is, at this Time, transporting large Armies of foreign Mercenaries to compleat the Works of Death, Desolation, and Tyranny, already begun with Circumstances of Cruelty and Perfidy scarcely paralleled in the most barbarous ages, and totally unworthy the Head of a civilized Nation.

He has constrained our Fellow Citizens, taken Captive on the high Seas, to bear Arms against their Country, to become the Executioners of their Friends and Brethren, or to fall themselves by their Hands.

He has excited Domestic Insurrections amongst us, and has endeavoured to bring on the Inhabitants of our Frontiers, the merciless Indian Savages, whose known Rule of Warfare, is an undistinguished Destruction of all Ages, Sexes, and Conditions.

In every Stage of these Oppressions we have petitioned for Redress, in the most humble Terms: Our repeated Petitions have been answered only by repeated Injury!—A Prince, whose Character is thus marked by every Act which may define a TYRANT, is unfit to be the Ruler of a FREE PEOPLE!

Nor have we been wanting in Attention to our British Brethren. We have warned them from Time to Time of Attempts by their Legislature to extend an unwarrantable Jurisdiction over us. We have reminded them of the Circumstances of our Emigration and Settlement here. We have appealed to their native Justice and Magnanimity, and we have conjured them by the Ties of our common Kindred to disavow these Usurpations, which would inevitably interrupt our Connexions and Correspondence. They too have been deaf to the Voice of Justice and of Consanguinity. We must, therefore, acquiesce in the Necessity which denounces our Separation, and hold them, as we hold the rest of Mankind, Enemies in War; in Peace, Friends.

We, therefore, the REPRESENTATIVES of the UNITED STATES OF AMERICA, in General Congress assembled, appealing to the SUPREME JUDGE of the World for the Rectitude of our Intentions, do, in the Name and by the Authority of the good People of these Colonies, solemnly Publish and Declare, That these United Colonies are, and of Right ought to be, FREE AND INDEPENDENT STATES; that they are absolved from all Allegiance to the British Crown; and that all political Connexion between them and the State of Great-Britain, is, and ought to be, totally dissolved;

The list of grievances. Complaints against the British King and the government

The final section of the document simply went on to explain that for all the reasons listed, the colonies were now to be free and independent states. They rejected British rule. They would no longer be loyal to King George III.

The resolution of independence by the United States

SELF-EVIDENT TRUTHS

Delegates of the Second Continental Congress leave Philadelphia's Independence Hall, July 4, 1776

The Declaration of Independence stands out in history not simply because it declared the colonies as independent of British rule and led to the formation of the United States of America, but because it recognized four truths that were "self-evident."

These truths would become the foundations of a new form of government. Jefferson claimed that he was not trying to create something original. He drew from many political thinkers and philosophers; rather, he was trying to recognize the spirit of the people and write what he thought were eternal truths.

Bronze statue of Thomas Jefferson writing the Declaration of Independence, Colonial Williamsburg, Virginia

These four truths are that everyone is equal, that people are born with natural rights that cannot be taken away, that governments are formed to protect these rights and gained power from the people and if the government violates any of these truths the people have a right to overthrow it.

The four truths of the Declaration of Independence

Four Noble Truths of the Declaration of Independence

WE HOLD THESE TRUTHS TO BE SELF-EVIDENT...

1. THAT ALL MEN ARE CREATED EQUAL

2. THAT THEY ARE ENDOWED BY THEIR CREATOR WITH CERTAIN UNALIENABLE RIGHTS, THAT AMONG THESE ARE *Life, Liberty* AND *the pursuit of Happiness*

3. THAT TO SECURE THESE RIGHTS, GOVERNMENTS ARE INSTITUTED AMONG MEN, *deriving their just powers* FROM THE *consent of the governed*

4. THAT WHENEVER ANY FORM OF GOVERNMENT BECOMES DESTRUCTIVE OF THESE ENDS, IT IS THE RIGHT OF THE PEOPLE TO ALTER OR TO ABOLISH IT, AND TO INSTITUTE NEW GOVERNMENT

July 4, 1776

The first right is written as *"all men are created equal."* While this is an ideal truth to strive towards, in practice people question if that was true at the time the Declaration of Independence was signed.

While "all men" referred to all of humankind, men and women were not treated as equal under the law. Another problem is that slavery was permitted in the colonies.

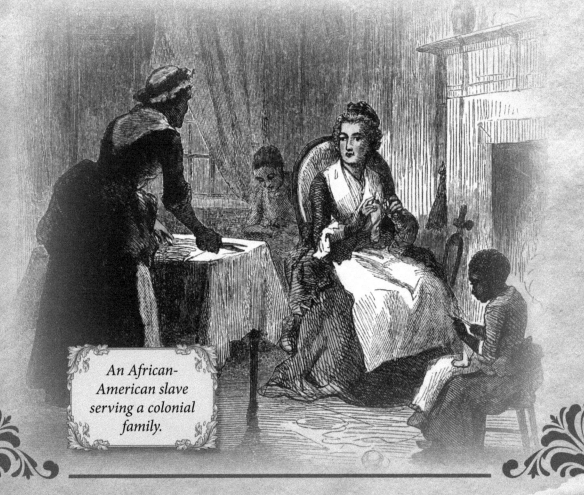

An African-American slave serving a colonial family.

In fact, Thomas Jefferson, who wrote that everyone should be treated as equal, owned slaves himself. Under the law, slaves were considered property and not people. This did not change even after the revolution. It took some time.

Thomas Jefferson welcomed by his slaves upon his return home to Monticello from Paris

However, Americans have strived, and continue to strive, towards ensuring the government recognizes and protects these truths that it is supposed to embody.

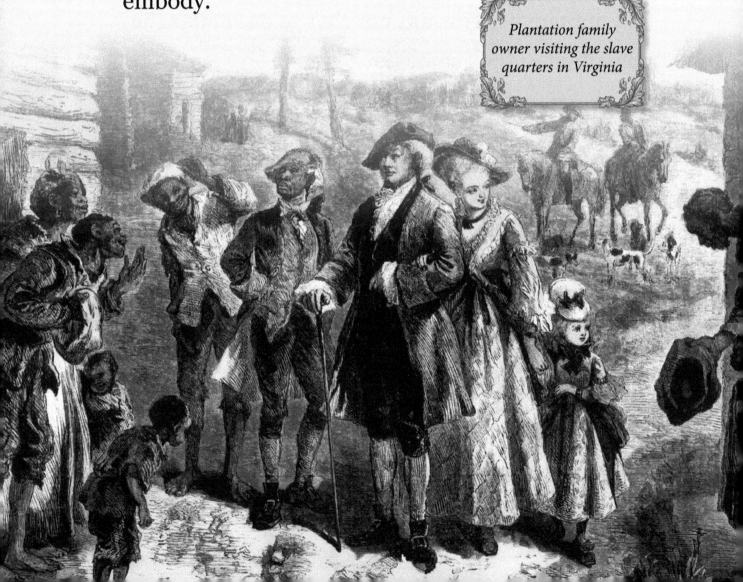

Plantation family owner visiting the slave quarters in Virginia

Slavery is now recognized as immoral and illegal, and laws are not supposed to discriminate based upon male or female. That does not mean that all issues have been resolved, however.

Freed slaves after the Emancipation Proclamation, 1863

There are many controversial political issues even today that touch upon the truth that everyone is equal. These issues question if our government truly protects all humans the way it is supposed to protect us.

Group of activists demonstrating against unemployment, taxes, and other political and social issues

Even now, every citizen is expected to hold the government accountable when it fails to live up to the standards to which it is required.

Protesting holding signs on Capitol Hill demanding the impeachment of a government official.

The second truth discusses the **unalienable rights.** Unalienable means that it cannot be given or taken away. It holds that every human being is born with certain things that they should, by nature, have. These rights are *the right to life, the right to liberty, and the right to pursue happiness.*

There are many things that are implied in these rights. The right to life means that everyone has a right to defend themselves from unjust attacks, (and by extension the right to revolt if their freedoms are taken away).

An image showing a concept of freedom

An image showing a concept on freedom of speech

Also implied in the right to liberty is freedom of speech and freedom of religion.

The right to pursue happiness does not mean that everyone is supposed to be happy, but it does mean that everyone should be allowed to make their own decisions regarding what they want to do in their life. It also includes the right to own property and to ensure one's own well-being.

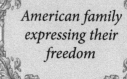

American family expressing their freedom

Crowd of people celebrating Independence Day

Many of these rights have overlapping principles. In the end, they mean that people have a right to live the best life as they see fit, so long as they do not take away anyone else's rights in the process. Everyone should be free.

These rights to protect oneself leads directly into the next truth which is that, in order to ensure that these fundamental rights are protected, governments should be established. These governments must derive their authority from the people they serve.

The governments must derive their authority from the people they serve

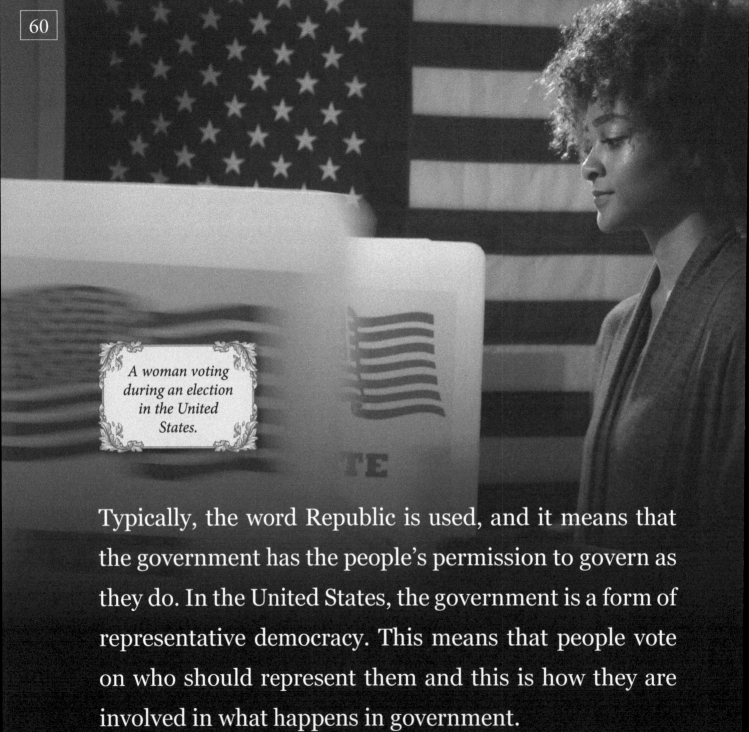

A woman voting during an election in the United States.

Typically, the word Republic is used, and it means that the government has the people's permission to govern as they do. In the United States, the government is a form of representative democracy. This means that people vote on who should represent them and this is how they are involved in what happens in government.

The final truth is that of a *people's right to revolution if the government stops serving the interests of the people and protecting their rights.*

Revolution is not something to be done lightly, but if peaceful means fail, it is necessary.

Revolution is necessary if peaceful resolution fails

The colonists were unable to resolve the situation with the British government peacefully, so they were forced to revolt.

The Battle of Lexington and Concord, 1775

Revolutions should only happen as a last resort and for a good cause. In worst situations though, like during the American Revolution, it is the duty of people to overthrow injustice and restore things to the way they should be.

American Revolution, Battle of Long Island, 1776

Jefferson's writing on these self-evident truths has proven to be inspiring into the present day.

Thomas Jefferson Memorial at Missouri History Museum in St. Louis, Missouri, USA

IN CONGRE

e unanimous Declaration of the

When in the course of human events, it becomes necessary

ng the powers of the earth, the separate and equal station to which the Laws of Nature and

re the causes which impel them to the separation. ———————— We hold these

unalienable Rights, that among these are Life, Liberty and the pursuit of Happin

the consent of the governed, — That whenever any Form of Government becomes destru

laying its foundation on such principles and organizing its powers in such form

long established should not be changed for light and transient cau

lishing the forms to which they are accustom

their duty, to

The Declaration of Independence has been recognized as one of the greatest documents in human history. The ideas Jefferson spoke of and his manner of expression have even been used to help explain revolutions that have occurred in other countries as people sought their freedoms.

The declaration of Independence of the United States

He seems to have been successful in writing something that would resonate across boundaries with the human heart.

Visit

www.speedypublishing.com

to download Free Baby Professor eBooks and view our

catalog of new and exciting Children's Books

Lightning Source UK Ltd.
Milton Keynes UK
UKHW051328040121
376379UK00002B/79